Our Lady of La Salette

A Mother Weeps for Her Children

PATRICE FAGNANT-MACARTHUR

ISBN 978-1-68901-939-2

Our Lady of La Salette

A Mother Weeps for Her Children

TABLE OF CONTENTS

INTRODUCTION

Our Lady of La Salette was trying to get my attention. It started in the days following the tragic fire at Notre Dame Cathedral in France. Someone posted on Facebook that there was a Marian apparition that had predicted this. Another person responded that it was Our Lady of La Salette. While I had heard of this title for the Blessed Mother, I knew nothing about it. Intrigued, I searched for her message and quickly found a terrifying apocalyptic prediction. I wondered why more wasn't known about this approved apparition. Why wasn't this common knowledge in Catholic circles the way Our Lady of Lourdes or Our Lady of Fatima are?

My parish library had three books on Our Lady of La Salette. I took out one that looked interesting and quickly read it. It offered information about the apparition that took place on September 19, 1846 but said nothing about the frightening secret I had read online. I was confused.

A few days letter, an article appeared in the National Catholic Register on Our Lady of La Salette and the site of the apparition in Corps, France.[1] I went back to my parish library and took out the other two books as well as undertook a considerable amount of online research. While I had no hope of making a pilgrimage to France, I made plans to visit

1

the National Shrine of Our Lady of La Salette in Attleboro, Massachusetts.

The more I learned, the more I realized that there was a story here — a message that our Blessed Mother wanted people to hear — a message that is just as relevant in our own day as it was in 1846. In this short book, I endeavor to weed out fact from fiction regarding this apparition and to share this important message from heaven. I trust that the Blessed Mother will help it get into the hands of those who need to hear it.

Our Lady of La Salette, Pray for Us.

The Feast of the Assumption

August 15, 2019

CHAPTER ONE
THE APPARITION

In 1846, the people of the small town of Corps, located in the French Alps, had largely forgotten God. Sunday Mass drew a small handful of people; most people treated Sunday as a day like any other. Both children and adults swore and cussed. There was no fasting and abstinence, even during Lent.

Maximin Giraud was 11 years old, small for his age but healthy. His father, Germain Giraud, was a wheelwright and carpenter who drank heavily. Maximin's mother had died, but his father had remarried. An active child, Maximin's "attention never stayed fixed for long; he could not concentrate; he darted about ceaselessly and so did his mind."[2] This description leads one to believe that if he were a child today, Maximin might be diagnosed with ADHD. He had never been to school and could barely recite the Our Father and Hail Mary. His father took Maximin to the café where he taught him how to smoke and drink. For the most part, Maximin "roamed the town at will . . . his mongrel dog Loulou tagging at his heels . . . He collected dung along the heavily travelled highway, or he kept an eye on the family's goat and ewe."[3]

On September 13, 1846, Pierre Selme made his way to Corps. He was a farmer from La Salette, a parish with a few hamlets. He was in search of a child to temporarily watch over his four cows. Maximin was hired to go for a week. His father negotiated the terms. Maximin would be paid as well as receive butter and cheese for his work.

Melanie Mathieu, age 14, was also from Corps, but she and Maximin had never met. One of eight poor children, she begged as a small child before being hired out when she was seven or eight years old to help care for babies. When she was a bit older, she worked as farm help. By 1846, she was considered a professional herder and was employed by Baptiste Pra. She was undersize, quiet, and fearful. Like Maximin, she knew her Our Father and Hail Mary, but she also knew some small bits of catechism that her mother had tried to teach her. She also had a basic concept of saints. Yet, she had only been to church a few times in her life and had never made her first communion; most Sundays she could be found tending her cows just as she did every other day.

Maximin and Melanie met on September 17, 1846 while tending their animals. Two days later, they would experience the apparition that would change their lives forever. It was noon on September 19th. The children were in a desolate mountain spot of La Salette, frequented only by the shepherds of the region. The Angelus bells rang and they took their animals to a place known as the "fountain", a drinking place in a nearby ravine. After eating lunch, the children fell asleep. This was most unusual. Melanie usually

4

always kept a watchful eye on the animals under her care. She woke up with a start an hour or two later. Where were the animals? She woke Maximin and the two searched for the cows. After they successfully found them, the children returned to the ravine to grab their knapsacks. It was then that Melanie first saw a great circle of light. She called Maximin to come see it.

The globe continued to grow until it was the size of a person. Melanie noticed a pair of hands first. In her words:

> I had hardly noticed the pair of hands become increasingly white when, instantly, I saw arms and sleeves down to the elbows resting as it were upon the knees. I also saw part of the dress below the elbows – it was brilliant with pearls. I saw before us, upon the stones, as it were, a woman who sat there weeping, her face buried in her hands and her elbows resting upon her knees but I could not see her face nor the rest of her body because the brightness was a hindrance.[4]

Both children carried shepherd sticks. Surprised by this vision, Melanie dropped hers, but Maximin held on to his, planning to use it as a weapon in case the woman did them any harm. Melanie feared it was a devil coming to get her. As soon as the woman began to speak, their fear left them. "They were fully reassured and felt, as it were, irresistibly attracted to this Lady."[5] The woman wept the entire time she

5

spoke to them. Maximin wanted to help her. He believed that she was hurt by either her son or husband.

The Lady shared the following message with them:

"Come near, my children, be not afraid; I am here to tell you great news.

"If my people will not submit, I shall be forced to let fall the arm of my Son. It is so strong, so heavy, that I can no longer withhold it.

"For how long a time do I suffer for you! If I would not have my Son abandon you, I am compelled to pray to him without ceasing; and as to you, you take not heed of it.

"However much you pray, however much you do, you will never recompense the pains I have taken for you.

"Six days I have given you to labor, the seventh I have kept for myself; and they will not give it to me. It is this which makes the arm of my Son so heavy.

"Those who drive the carts cannot swear without introducing the name of my Son. These are the two things which make the arm of my Son so heavy.

"If the harvest is spoilt, it is all on your account. I gave you warning last year with the potatoes ('pommes de terre') but you did not heed it. On the contrary, when you found the potatoes spoilt, you swore, you took the name of my Son in vain. They will continue to decay, so that by Christmas there will be none left."

The French expression "pommes de terre" intrigued Melanie. In the local dialect the word for potatoes was "las truffas", whereas "pommes" for Melanie meant the fruit of the apple tree. Hence she instinctively turned towards Maximin to ask for an explanation, but the Beautiful Lady forestalled her.

"Ah, my children, you do not understand? Well, wait, I shall say it otherwise."

And she continued her discourse in the local dialect of their region.

"If you have wheat, it is no good to sow it; all you sow the insects will eat, and what comes up will fall into dust when you thresh it."

"There will come a great famine. Before the famine comes, the children under seven years of age will be seized with trembling and will die in the hands of those who hold them; the others will do penance by the famine. The walnuts will become bad, and the grapes will rot."

Here the Beautiful Lady addressed the children separately, confiding to each a secret. She spoke first to Maximin, and though the little shepherd did not perceive that her tone of voice had changed, Melanie at his side could not hear a word, though she still saw the Beautiful Lady's lips moving. Then came Melanie's turn to receive her secret under like conditions. Both secrets were given in French.

Again addressing the two children in the idiom familiar to them, the Lady continued: "If they are converted, the stones and rocks will change into mounds of wheat, and the potatoes will be self-sown in the land.

8

"Do you say your prayers well, my children?" she asked the shepherds. Both answered with complete frankness: "Not very well, Madam."

"Ah, my children", she exhorted them, "you must be sure to say them well morning and evening. When you cannot do better, say at least an Our Father and a Hail Mary; but when you have time, say more."

"There are none who go to Mass except a few aged women. The rest work on Sunday all summer; then in the winter, when they know not what to do, they go to Mass only to mock at religion. During Lent, they go to the meat-market like dogs."

"Have you never seen wheat that is spoilt, my children?" the Beautiful Lady then asked them. "No, Madam", they replied.

"But you, my child", she insisted, addressing the little boy in particular, "you must surely have seen some once when you were at the farm of Coin with your father. (Coin was a hamlet near the town of Corps). The owner of the field told your father to go and see his ruined wheat. You went together. You took two or three ears of wheat into your hands and rubbed them, and they fell into dust. Then you continued home. When you were still half an hour's distance from Corps, your father gave you a piece of bread and said to you: 'Here, my child, eat some bread this year at least; I don't know who will eat any next year, if the wheat goes on like that.'"

Confronted with such precise details, Maximin eagerly replied: "Oh yes, Madam, I remember now; just at this moment I did not remember."

Then the Lady, again speaking French as at the beginning of her discourse and when giving the secrets, said to them: "Well, my children, you will make this known to all my people."

Now she turned slightly to her left, passed in front of the children, crossed the brook Sezia, stepping on stones emerging from it, and when she was about ten feet from the opposite bank repeated her final request, without turning around or stopping: "Well, my children, you will make this well known to all my people."[6]

The children found it hard to gaze directly at the apparition due to the brightness of the great light. As the Lady went up to heaven, she gazed earthward. Melanie's eyes met hers. "She was no longer weeping but a profound sadness marked her features."[7]

The apparition lasted approximately half an hour, even though to the children the time passed quickly. There were other shepherds present on the mountain that day, but none of them saw the light of the apparition. Maximin's dog was also unaffected by the apparition. Despite being a keen watchdog, Loulou slept peacefully through the whole experience a step or two behind the children, even as the light enveloped him. The children did not know who had visited them. Melanie thought she might be a great saint. They began to refer to her as the "Beautiful Lady".

Melanie and Maximin heard the message more with their hearts than with their ears. At times, the Lady spoke in proper French, which neither child knew much of. At other times, she spoke in their local dialect. "They retained all of it perfectly, the French as well as the dialect, whether or not they understood everything."[8] For the rest of their lives, they would not forget.

CHAPTER TWO
AFTER THE APPARITION

When Maximin returned to Selme's home, he told his employer what had happened. Selme decided to question Melanie; her story agreed with the boy's version. It was Grandmother Pra at Melanie's home who first identified the "Beautiful Lady" as the Blessed Virgin. The adults quickly decided that the children needed to share the story with Fr. Jacques Perrin who was in charge of the parish of La Salette.

The next day, the children set off early in the morning to visit with Fr. Perrin. En route, they encountered a constable who questioned them about their errand. The constable responded with derisive laughter, but decided this news was something the mayor needed to hear.

Meanwhile, the children reached the rectory where the door was answered by the housekeeper, Françoise. She took her job as gatekeeper for the priest seriously and was not going to allow the priest to be disturbed. Faced with no other choice, the children shared their story with her. Little did they know that Fr. Perrin was in the next room, listening intently to all that they said. Like the Beautiful Lady herself, Fr. Perrin responded to the children's recounting of her message with tears.

It was time for Maximin to return home to his father now that his term of employment was completed. Selme escorted him home. Selme found Giraud at the local tavern, where he explained to Maximin's father what had happened. Giraud's fellow patrons were quick to poke fun at him and this pious matter his son seemed to be caught up in.

For his part, Maximin did not bother staying home with his stepmother; instead he rushed to see his grandmother. He knew that she would be happy to see him after his time away. When she asked how his time had been, he retold all that happened. His grandmother had never heard the boy tell such a story. It was so out of character for Maximin that she knew that he must be telling the truth. How fortunate that her grandson had been so blessed! She quickly shared the news with her friends. They rushed to see Maximin and he was forced to retell the story over and over.

Exhausted by the day's events, Maximin went home and went to sleep, only to be rudely awakened by his angry drunk father pulling him out of bed. His father demanded that Maximin explain what all this foolishness was about. The weary Maximin began once more to tell of the Beautiful Lady and her message. As Maximin began to share the first words of the Lady's message, Giraud was flabbergasted. How could his ignorant son know such things? He had never been able to learn much of anything. It was too much for his drunken

14

mind to comprehend. He sent everyone back to bed. Perhaps by the next day all would be forgotten.

After the children left the rectory at La Salette and Maximin had departed to go home, Melanie decided to go to Mass. She very rarely attended Mass, but after hearing the Lady's message, it seemed important to go. Much to her surprise, Fr. Perrin shared the story of all that had happened to her and Maximin from the pulpit. His words were confused. He spoke through tears. The parishioners could barely make out what he was saying, much less understand it. But Melanie did, and so did the mayor who also happened to be sitting in the congregation.

Mayor Peytard had heard the unbelievable tale from the constable. He had quickly dismissed the story as a childish prank not to be given any credence. What was the good priest doing sharing this story from the pulpit? Even if, by some miracle, the story was true, the mayor knew that this was not how the Church worked. The matter needed careful investigation before any sort of pronouncement was made. The other people in the pews may have been confused at the moment, but they would soon understand. The mayor could only envision the uproar that was about to take over his quiet community. He had to put a stop to this foolishness before the matter got out of hand.

Melanie ran home after Mass, eager to escape to the peace of Ablandins, but her peace would be short-lived. Mayor Peytard headed to her home that afternoon. After sharing some small talk with Baptiste Pra, he began to question Melanie, asking her to share what had happened on the mountain. Mayor Peytard was determined to catch the girl in a lie. He deliberately contradicted her and questioned her in multiple ways, hoping to entrap her. He threatened her, telling her she would be a laughing-stock among her friends. When that didn't work, he said that if she did not deny the story, he would have her thrown into jail. She still remained firm. Finally he offered her three months wages to keep quiet. It was tempting to the impoverished child. What a blessing that money would be for her family! But, still she refused, telling the mayor, "You could give me this whole house full of crowns, and still you would not stop me from saying what I have seen and heard."[9]

Having witnessed this whole encounter, Baptiste Pra decided that the story of the vision was worth writing down. This was most unusual in this time and place. Pra struggled with both writing and spelling, but he recorded all that had happened for the world to know.

Having struck out with Melanie, Mayor Peytard decided his next target would be Maximin. Perhaps he could be more successful with the young boy. The mayor arrived at the

Giraud home early Monday morning. This time, the mayor didn't even pretend to be kind. He immediately began to threaten Maximin with prison if he did not recant the story. The boy was as faithful to his story as Melanie had been. The mayor soon realized he was getting nowhere with his tactics. Instead, he insisted that he and Melanie both join him the following Sunday at the place where the vision was alleged to have taken place. Then, they would get to the bottom of this nonsense and dispense of this story once and for all.

On Saturday, September 26th, Melanie visited Corps to see her father, a man who was as eager to believe the story of the apparition as Giraud had been. Fr. Mélin was the parish priest of Corps as well as the archpriest of that area (the bishop's representative). While no one had spoken to him directly of the apparition, he had heard of it and was eager to speak to both Melanie and Maximin. When he noticed that Melanie was in town, he summoned both children to come and see him.

He interviewed the children separately and then together, cross-examining them. He kept a stoic appearance, offering no indication of his thoughts on the matter. He demanded that the children accompany him on Monday the 28th on a visit to the mountain. This would mean a difficult and long journey for the children two days in a row as they were already obligated to visit the mountain the following day with the mayor, but the children offered no objection. They did as they were told.

Indeed, the children were happy to once again be in the place of the apparition when they went with the mayor. They eagerly demonstrated where everything happened. The mayor once again tried a show of force, hoping to put an end to the story. A constable had accompanied the group; he produced a rope and threatened to tie up Maximin and drag him to prison. He still would not deny the story. The mayor soon realized the children were not pretending. Whether it was real or not, the children believed that they had witnessed a vision.

The following day the children repeated the journey with Fr. Mélin and five other people brought along to be objective observers. Melanie and Maximin once again retold the story, pointing out all the important places. The priest soon became convinced that the children were telling the truth but he said nothing. Before they left, one member of the party suggested that they pray. Fr. Mélin agreed and the group knelt and said the rosary. They also noticed that the spring, which was usually dried out at that time of year, was now flowing freely. Fr. Mélin took an empty wine bottle and filled it with water from the spring.

Fr. Mélin was now convinced of the authenticity of the apparition but kept silent. His job was not to endorse the apparition, but rather to report what had happened to the bishop.

Fr. Mélin had decided to give some of the water from the spring to one of his parishioners who had been ill for a long time. Mme. Anglot began a novena to Our Lady and drank of the water for nine days. She was unable to eat anything else but was able to take the water without difficulty. On the ninth day, she was able to get out of bed and eat heartily. Fr. Mélin refused to call it a miracle, but did admit the whole matter was extraordinary. It was most definitely time to write to the bishop and put the matter into his capable hands.

CHAPTER THREE
THE BISHOP SPEAKS

Bishop Philibert de Bruillard was 81 years old. He had been ordained at the age of 24 and then served as a professor of philosophy and theology at the seminary of St. Sulpice in Paris. During the French Revolution, he had continued to minister in secret. Later, he served as a parish priest before being consecrated as a bishop. By the time of the vision of La Salette, he had been the pastoral leader of Grenoble for 25 years. He was known as a man of "sterling faith" and "notable piety".[10] Fr. Mélin had no doubt that the bishop would take the matter seriously and conduct a thorough investigation.

Upon receiving Fr. Mélin's initial letter, the bishop sent a letter to all the priests of his diocese forbidding them from speaking or publishing anything about the vision until he or the Vatican made a decision regarding their authenticity. Despite this imposed silence, word of the vision was spreading. Fr. Mélin kept up a steady correspondence with the bishop regarding the events in Corps and La Salette, but so did many others. The bishop had a pile of letters from both officials and common people; everyone had an opinion of what he should do.

In mid-October, Bishop de Bruillard chose several of his most trusted advisors to investigate. Father Chambon was superior of the minor seminary. He was accompanied by three members of the seminary faculty. The bishop expected a full report in his hands by November 10th. He then appointed two commissions to sift through all the information he had received. One was made up of eight canons of the cathedral. The other was comprised of six professors of the Grenoble major seminary. They were to operate independently of each other and offer their own evaluation of the material.

While the bishop was investigating and mulling over the situation, the local people took matters into their own hands. Many began to make pilgrimages to the mountain where the vision took place. Melanie and Maximin were never left in peace. Everyone wanted to speak with them. Many offered them money (which they always refused). Maximin's father began to be interested in getting to the bottom of what had happened to his son, especially after Maximin told him that the lady had spoken of Giraud as well. Maximin's grandmother wanted to make the trip to the mountain and his stepmother asked for permission from Giraud to go with her. He agreed, directing his wife to look carefully to see if there were any signs that the children might have been tricked in some way.

When she returned, Giraud's wife spoke favorably of the location and urged her husband to go see it for himself.

Perhaps he could even be cured of the asthma that he suffered from. At first Giraud would not commit to going, but he freely allowed his son to return. He even made a wooden cross at Maximin's request that his son wanted to put on the mountain. A short time later, Giraud did make the journey. He prayed for healing and drank some of the water from the spring. He experienced a complete conversion. Not only was he physically healed of his difficulty in breathing, he began to practice his faith with all his heart. Upon returning to the town, he immediately went to confession. He took part at Mass and in the sacraments. He ceased spending his days in the tavern. He even worked on controlling his temper. He was a new man, inside and out. He lived as a faithful Catholic until his death three years later.

Giraud was not the only one to be converted. The people had heard that the Blessed Mother was crying due to their behavior. Fr. Mélin was quick to acknowledge the change in his parishioners. No longer did they treat Sunday as just another day of work. They attended Mass and went to confession and communion. Swearing and vulgar language were now rarely heard.

On November 17th, the people conducted the first organized pilgrimage to the mountain. Over 600 people took part. One parishioner who wanted very much to go but was unable to do so was Marie Laurent, wife of the town baker. She was forty-eight years old and had been unable to walk without crutches for several years due to rheumatism. Even that was painful and she was unable to attend church. She had been drinking some of the La Salette water and making a novena asking for the intercession of Our Blessed Mother to help heal her. She begged those going on the pilgrimage to pray for her. The pilgrims obliged, calling out to God while they were on the mountain to please heal her. When the pilgrims returned from their journey, Mrs. Laurent rushed out to meet them. She could walk! Not only that, she could run! The time she was healed was the exact time the pilgrims had prayed for her on the mountain.

News of the healing spread and a second pilgrimage was scheduled for November 28th. This time, more than a thousand pilgrims braved snow and freezing cold to climb the mountain.

Bishop de Bruillard became concerned about Melanie and Maximin's welfare. Fr. Mélin agreed that something should be done. The two decided that the children should be sent to school with the Sisters of Providence in Corps. Melanie would live there and Maximin would be a day student with the diocese of Grenoble paying for any expense incurred.

In December, the two commissions reported to the bishop. They both came to the same conclusion: take a wait and see approach. They felt that there was not yet enough evidence to either endorse or reject the apparition. The bishop agreed to abide by their decision.

By this point, news of the apparition had reached Paris and the official government was not pleased. Word was sent from Paris that "the concocters of the pretended apparition were to be found and punished."[11] The Royal Prosecutor at Grenoble traveled to Ablandins where he interrogated Baptiste Pra and Pierre Selme. He took with him the written account that Pra had made of the children's testimony.

In the spring, the Justice of the Peace of Corps was directed to interview the children. Fr. Mélin had faith that the children's story would stand up under questioning and urged them not to be afraid. The interview lasted six hours and turned up no new information.

In June, the Minister of Justice and of Cults wrote to Bishop de Bruillard, demanding that he stop the spread of information about the apparition. The bishop responded that he had, in fact, forbidden preaching or publication on the matter.

In response to the growing notoriety of the vision, Bishop de Bruillard began a juridical inquiry into the apparition on July 19, 1847. Two priests were put in charge: Father Rousselot, a professor of theology who would become the official historian of La Salette, and Father Orcel, superior of the major seminary.

September 19, 1847 was the first anniversary of the apparition. There was still no official word from the Church as to its authenticity, but the bishop did allow Mass to be offered on the mountain. By September 17th, throngs of people were making their way to the mountain. The local churches were packed. Priests heard confessions for hours. There was no lodging to be had anywhere. Many pilgrims decided to simply stay on the mountain itself, despite a furious storm that was raging. At 2:30 a.m. Mass was offered on the two altars that had been set up on the mountain. When those Masses were complete, another set of Masses began. This continued until noon. Around 10 a.m. the sun came out.

Maximin and Melanie were there among the fifty to sixty thousand people who had come to pray. They were encouraged to retell the story. And so they did, one line at a time. In this time before microphones and speakers, they would say their part, and then others would repeat it until it traveled through the crowd. At the end of the day, the children led the pilgrims in praying the Rosary.

In October, Father Rousselot and Father Orcel reported to the bishop that, after investigating all the evidence including twenty-three cures attributed to Our Lady of La Salette, they were convinced that the apparition was authentic. The bishop, a patient and prudent man, then sent that report to a commission of 16 priests who went over it line by line, debating every point. In the end, twelve of them agreed that the apparition was true; four dissented.

Bishop de Bruillard would sign a formal doctrinal pronouncement on La Salette on the fifth anniversary of the apparition, September 19, 1851. It was then sent to Rome where Cardinal Lambruschini studied and approved it. On November 16th, the document was read at the 600 churches under Bishop de Bruillard's care.

In the pronouncement, the bishop asserted:

> Haste on our part would not only have been contrary to the prudence with the great Apostle recommends to a bishop; it would also have served to buttress the prejudices of the enemies of our religion and of a great many Catholics who are Catholics only in name. While a multitude of pious souls warmly welcomed this reputed apparition as a fact, we again and again considered with care all the grounds which could lead us to reject it. . .

> On the other hand, we were strictly obliged not to regard as impossible an event which the Lord (who would dare deny it?) might well have permitted to further His glory, for His arm is not shortened and His power is the same today as in ages past.

27

In conclusion, the document stated, "We give judgment that the apparition of the Blessed Virgin to two herders on September 19, 1846, on the mountain of the Alpine chain situated in the parish of La Salette in the territory of the archpriest of Corps, bears in itself all the marks of truth, and the faithful have grounds to believe it indubitable and certain."[12]

The Church had spoken, but the controversy surrounding Our Lady of La Salette was far from over.

CHAPTER FOUR
THE SEERS AND THE SECRETS

During their time on the mountain of La Salette, the Blessed Mother revealed two secrets – one each to Melanie and Maximin. The children were not aware of the contents of each other's secrets. They had both been instructed not to share them and they honored Our Lady's request.

Cardinal de Bonald of Lyon, like many others, was very curious about what those secrets might contain. As a consulter to the pope, he had the power to do something about it. In June of 1851, he sent a letter to Bishop de Bruillard requesting that the seers tell him their secrets so that he might then pass them along to the Holy Father. The bishop agreed that the Holy Father should be informed of the secrets, but he wanted to do it directly, without the cardinal acting as middle-man.

The children were not easily convinced to share their secrets with the pope. After all, they had been sworn to secrecy by Our Blessed Mother herself. Such a confidence was not to be easily broken. The bishop's envoy discussed the matter with Maximin. After some time, Maximin agreed that if the pope, the Vicar of Christ, asked for the secret, he would give it to him.

At the bishop's house, Maximin began to write down the secret, only to move too enthusiastically and knock over the container of ink. The paper was ruined. He had to start again. He took more care with the second attempt. When he was finished, the bishop showed him how to fold the paper and place it inside an envelope. The bishop then sealed the envelope with molten wax. Two priests signed the envelope as witnesses.

It took three attempts to convince Melanie to reveal her secret. In the end, it was Fr. Rousselot who convinced her to do so. In the course of writing her secret, she asked for the meaning of the word "infallibly". Later she asked what the term "anti-Christ" meant. Like Maximin, she put the secret into an envelope that was then sealed by the bishop. Later, she remembered a date that she should have included and asked to go to the bishop in order to make the correction. She was given this permission and, after adding this information, felt satisfied.

The bishop sent Fr. Rousselot and Fr. Gerin to Rome with the two secrets along with a letter asking for the pope's opinion of the apparitions. Bishop de Bruillard agreed to abide by the pope's decision.

On July 18, the two priests met with Pope Pius IX. He read the secrets. He smiled while he read Maximin's but his response to Melanie's was more grave. He said, "Calamities threaten France. But she is not the only one to blame. Italy is, too, and Germany and Switzerland and all Europe. It is not without reason that the Church is called militant."[13] He told the two priests that he would study the secrets further and then respond to them.

Pope Pius IX met with Fr. Rousselot again on August 22nd. The pope said that the bishop was free to make whatever pronouncement about the apparition that he felt was appropriate. As of the date of this writing, the secrets have never been officially revealed by the Vatican.

Seeing a vision of Our Lady does not automatically make a person a canonized saint. Those who have been blessed with such a vision and then canonized, such as St. Catherine Laboure (Our Lady of the Miraculous Medal), St. Bernadette (Our Lady of Lourdes), and Saints Jacinta and Francisco (Our Lady of Fatima), were canonized due to the virtue of their lives after the apparitions took place. While one might presume that those chosen for such an honor as a visit from Our Lady would have special help from God to live holy lives, all humans retain the gift of free will.

Maximin's life after the bishop pronounced the vision authentic was one of restless searching. In keeping with his childhood personality, he could not stay in one place for long. He attempted to become a priest and entered the seminary, but he was not academically inclined. He thought he might become a doctor or pharmacist, but that too did not work out. He ended up working a string of menial jobs and was often destitute and hungry. He decided to go to Rome where he became a papal zouave (part of the infantry force designed to defend the Papal States). He served for six months before returning to France. In 1870, he was recruited to fight for France in the Prussian war; he never saw battle, instead serving his time in the Grenoble barracks. By this time, he was thirty-five years old and, like his father before him, suffered from asthma.

Throughout his life, Maximin struggled, never finding a place where he belonged. By all accounts, he was unsuccessful in the world's eyes. It had been reported that he got drunk easily, but he did not drink much. It is suspected that he most likely had an intolerance of alcohol that made him get tipsy after only having a small amount. Unfortunately, he had the misfortune of living in a place where wine was served with every meal. Despite his professional and personal challenges, he always remained faithful to Our Blessed Mother. He strove to live a life of virtue. A comrade in the zouave testified that Maximin had no patience for off-color jokes or behavior.

On November 11, 1865, the newspaper *La Vie Parisienne* published an article saying that Maximin no longer believed in the apparition. Maximin sued for libel. The case was settled out of court and an apology was printed in the paper. Maximin responded by publishing a seventy-two page booklet, *My Profession of Faith in the Apparition of La Salette*.[14]

Maximin died at the age of forty. La Salette water was his last drink and the Eucharist his last food.[15] Maximin had the final word on his life and the apparition in his last will and testament:

> I believe in all that the holy, apostolic, Roman Church teaches, in everything defined by our Holy Father, the Pope, the august and infallible Pius IX. I firmly believe, even were it to cost the shedding of my blood, in the renowned apparition of the Blessed Virgin on the holy mountain of La Salette, September 19, 1846, the apparition to which I have testified in words, works, in writings, in suffering. After my death let no one assert that he has heard me make any retraction concerning the great event of La Salette, for in lying to the world he would be lying in his own breast. With these sentiments, I give my heart to Our Lady of La Salette.[16]

Unlike Maximin who died young, Melanie lived to be seventy-two. Like Maximin, she attempted to enter religious life. In fact, she attempted this several times, moving from convent to convent, but never making her vows. Melanie had been a shy child who did not like to be in the spotlight. With time, however, she came to thrive on the adulation of pilgrims. She could not live a quiet life as a religious sister and struggled to obey her superiors.

She also ended up living a wandering life, bouncing frequently between France and Italy. She wrote a largely fictional autobiography in which she claimed to have had extraordinary piety and mystical experiences in childhood, despite all evidence to the contrary. Melanie needed people to honor her and pay attention to her and was willing to tell them what they wanted to hear in order to have that continue. She began to tease people with information about the secret that Our Lady had revealed to her.

"In a series of letters to Abbé Félicien Bliard, beginning on December 26, 1870, Melanie made it clear that she had seen and felt, rather than heard, much of what she had related in the Secret, and that it was impossible to put everything fully into words, as she wrote:

> The Holy Virgin spoke all the words, either of the secrets, or of the rules, but I could only guess or penetrate the rest of what she said in words: a great veil was lifted, events were uncovered to my eyes and to my imagination as She spoke all the words and a great space was opened before me; I saw events, the changes in the operation of the earth, and the unchanging God in His glory watching the Virgin, who lowered Herself to speak to two peasants. . ."[17]

In 1879, Melanie published a booklet with the imprimatur of Bishop Salvtore Luigi Zola entitled *Apparition of the Blessed Virgin on the Mountain of La Salette*. This version of the secret is much longer than the one Melanie wrote for the pope in 1851 and contains much more detail. In 1923, this booklet was put on the Index of Forbidden Books. As of 1966, the Index of Forbidden Books no longer exists. Unfortunately, this episode led many to believe that the apparition at La Salette as a whole was now rejected. That was not the case at all.

The 1879 version of the secret is widely available on the internet.[18] Indeed, that was the first thing I found when I searched for the message of Our Lady of La Salette. It is highly apocalyptic in nature and is best treated with skepticism. There are those who take this version of the secret as the word of Our Blessed Mother, including the prediction that Rome will suffer apostasy, and use it to argue that this is the case in the world today. This is most unfortunate. Melanie desired attention. She may have been suffering from some sort of mental illness. While one cannot be 100% certain, there is no reason to believe that Our Blessed Mother conveyed this longer, more specific secret.

Yet, despite Melanie's struggles with pride and her casual relationship with the truth, she did retain a great faith, attending Mass daily. She also never changed a word of her testimony about the original apparition. One can be confident that her reports of what happened on September 19, 1846 were true.

What about the original secrets from 1851? They had seemed to be lost. Father Jean Stem who had been an archivist of the Missionaries of La Salette, had tried to find the official version. The Congregation of the Faith had informed him that they could not be found. However, in 1998, Monsignor Bertone, then secretary of the Congregation of the Faith, opened the files of Pope Leo XIII to researchers.[19]

Father Michel Corteville found the original documents of the secrets among Pope Leo XIII's papers on October 2, 1999. They became "the subject of a doctoral thesis in theology which was supported by Fr. Corteville in 2000 at the Angelicum, the Pontifical University of the Dominicans. This thesis of more than 1000 pages was summarized in 2002 in a format more accessible to a wider audience, in a book published by Editions Fayard, under the title *Découverte du secret de La Salette* (*Discovery of the Secret of La Salette*) by Father Corteville and Father René Laurentin."[20] This book has not been published in English.

While the Vatican has not made any statement on the texts of these secrets, it seems reasonable to believe that these are the original secrets. The events described in these secrets are open to debate. As with all prophetic messages, the details are subject to change based on humanity's response to the call for conversion.

Maximin's Secret (written on July 3, 1851)

On September 19, 1846, we saw a beautiful Lady. We never said that this lady was the Blessed Virgin but we always said that it was a beautiful Lady.

I do not know if it is the Blessed Virgin or another person. As for me, I believe today that it is the Blessed Virgin.

Here is what this Lady said to me:

"If my people continue, what I will say to you will arrive earlier, if it changes a little, it will be a little later.

France has corrupted the universe, one day it will be punished. The faith will die out in France: three quarters of France will not practice religion anymore, or almost no more, the other part will practice it without really practicing it.

Then, after [that], nations will convert, the faith will be rekindled everywhere.

A great country, now Protestant, in the north of Europe, will be converted; by the support of this country all the other nations of the world will be converted.

Before all that arrives, great disorders will arrive, in the Church, and everywhere. Then, after [that], our Holy Father the Pope will be persecuted. His successor will be a pontiff that nobody expects.

Then, after [that], a great peace will come, but it will not last a long time. A monster will come to disturb it.

All that I tell you here will arrive in the other century, at the latest in the year two thousand."

Melanie's Secret (written on July 6, 1851)

J.M.J.

Secret which the Blessed Virgin gave me on the Mountain of La Salette on September 19, 1846

Mélanie, I will say something to you which you will not say to anybody:

The time of the God's wrath has arrived!

If, when you say to the people what I have said to you so far, and what I will still ask you to say, if, after that, they do not convert, (if they do not do penance, and they do not cease working on Sunday, and if they continue to blaspheme the Holy Name of God), in a word, if the face of the earth does not change, God will be avenged against the people ungrateful and slave of the demon.

My Son will make his power manifest! Paris, this city soiled by all kinds of crimes, will perish infallibly. Marseilles will be destroyed in a little time. When these things arrive, the disorder will be complete on the earth, the world will be given up to its impious passions.

The pope will be persecuted from all sides, they will shoot at him, they will want to put him to death, but no one will not be able to do it, the Vicar of God will triumph again this time.

The priests and the Sisters, and the true servants of my Son will be persecuted, and several will die for the faith of Jesus-Christ.

A famine will reign at the same time.

After all these will have arrived, many will recognize the hand of God on them, they will convert, and do penance for their sins.

A great king will go up on the throne, and will reign a few years. Religion will re-flourish and spread all over the world, and there will be a great abundance, the world, glad not to be lacking nothing, will fall again in its disorders, will give up God, and will be prone to its criminal passions.

[Among] God's ministers, and the Spouses of Jesus-Christ, there will be some who will go astray, and that will be the most terrible.

Lastly, hell will reign on earth. It will be then that the Antichrist will be born of a Sister, but woe to her! Many will believe in him, because he will claim to have come from heaven, woe to those who will believe in him!

39

That time is not far away, twice 50 years will not go by.

My child, you will not say what I have just said to you. (You will not say it to anybody, you will not say if you must say it one day, you will not say what that it concerns), finally you will say nothing anymore until I tell you to say it![21]

Chapter Five

The Blessed Mother's Message and its Importance for Today

Our Blessed Mother's apparition at La Salette was over 170 years ago. Does her message still matter for today? The answer is an unequivocal yes.

In examining the message of Our Lady of La Salette in more detail, let us first look at the message itself and its relevance in the context of the time in which it was given.

Our Lady of La Salette spoke in the name of God. In that respect, she followed the tradition of the Old Testament prophets. The Blessed Virgin is the "Queen of Prophets".[22] She is calling the people to return to God and repent of their sins. In this particular case, she was speaking out against Sunday work and blasphemy, violations of the second and third commandments: keep holy the Sabbath and do not take the Lord's name in vain. Indirectly, these are also violations of the first commandment because those who work on Sunday or take God's name in vain are not putting God before everything else as the first commandment directs us to do. These sins are the reason for her tears.

Our Lady of La Salette indicated that during the previous year (1845), there had been a poor potato crop. According to her, this had been a warning from God that the people should change their ways, but they did not heed the warning. Instead they blasphemed even more. Our Lady indicated that by the coming Christmas (of 1846) there would be almost no potatoes to be found. This proved to be the case. Not only France, but also Germany, England, and most especially Ireland suffered from a terrible potato famine.

The people of Corps did heed Our Lady's warnings and experienced a great conversion. After the years of 1846 and 1847, they had good harvests and only a minimal number of potatoes were affected by disease.[23]

Our Lady also foretold that the wheat crops would fail. "For several years after the Apparition, it was observed in certain localities that the wheat did almost literally fall into dust at threshing, or, at least, so little grain did it yield, that it seemed to melt under the flail. The ears of corn, which at first appeared fair and full, produced but few grains of wheat."[24]

She predicted that many children would be seized by trembling and that a great famine would follow. "During the years immediately following the Apparition of La Salette, a great number of children died from the effects of a strange epidemic."[25] "In 1847 there was a very unusual mortality among the children of Corps and nearby villages, and in 1854 great numbers were carried off by cholera, complicated by miliary fever (probably tuberculosis). These little victims were suddenly seized with a violent chill, began trembling all over and died after two or three hours of agony."[26]

As for the famine, many in Europe died due to food shortages in the years following the apparition. In 1855, "nearly one hundred thousand people had died of starvation in France alone! And according to conservative estimates, from 1854 to 1856 inclusively, as many as one million persons throughout Europe died victims of the same 'high price of food.'"[27]

In all of Our Lady's apparitions, her warnings are conditional. Like the prophets of old, she states that if the people do not repent, evils will befall them. The future is not set in stone. We do have the power to change the dire predictions for the future if we repent, pray for the conversion of sinners, and turn back to God.

Our Lady of La Salette commanded the children to what seemed like an impossible task. They were to make her message known to all the world. That mission continues today.

Back in 1953, Fr. James O'Reilly wrote:

> Never more than now have men so much needed the salutary teachings of La Salette. We look out on a world today that seems to be in complete revolt against all authority, human and divine. . . . The Christian principles that once ruled our lives and fostered obedience, modesty, and respect, have been repudiated as old-fashioned. In every department of

43

human activity, in the home, in business, in our national life, our educational system, all forms of entertainment, in music, literature and art, the seeds of revolt, irreverence, indecency and unbridled license have been cultivated, and now we are reaping the whirlwind in a national crime wave, in gross immorality, in an alarming breakdown of the marriage bond and of home life that seems unparalleled in nearly two thousand years of Christianity. . . [Our Lady's] tears still flow, her work of merciful intercession still goes on for a heedless world. What then, does she ask of each one of us? She pleads for our conversion, and in her gentle maternal way urges us all to lead lives of prayer, penance and reparation.[28]

How is it possible that those words were written in the 1950s, an era we now look back on as so conservative compared to our own? How much more in need is our world today when so many have turned their backs on God and religious practice?

Our Lady wants all of us to be reconciled to her Son. She wants this so much that she weeps for her children who have fallen away.

These tears are La Salette's most powerful unspoken message. The beautiful Lady weeps but she never refers to her tears, never so much as alludes to them. They are meant to speak for themselves and

44

they do. They are an unspoken message but they add a crucial dimension to her words . . . [The tears] are liquid sorrow, molten streams of pain running down the Lady's face and a very obvious show of love. . . [They] highlight the words and give urgency and crucial importance to the entire message. If someone from heaven, and the Blessed Virgin at that, is provoked to tears over disrespect for the Day of the Lord and the Name of Jesus, then the word is out that these offenses are more evil than people think they are and should be carefully avoided.[29]

How true that last statement is. How many people think nothing of skipping Mass (or never attend at all)? How often do we hear the name of the Lord used in vain? Truly, these acts matter to God.

Not honoring God in his Name and on his day, not worshiping, not praying are the root causes, the deep-seated sins against God that bring on those 'sins against the neighbor.' The Lady says, without actually pronouncing the words, that serving God and serving the neighbor are not two acts, but one.

On the face of it, the La Salette message is limited in its demands: Mass, prayer, penance, and respect for Christ's name appear to be the bare bones of religion . . . On the other hand, when these elements are observed well, they launch an intimate and powerful

45

Christian life, for all of Christian life is based on those demands.[30]

Our Blessed Mother took the people to task for not paying attention to the sorrow that they were causing her and her Son. "She also reproached her people for not seeing the signs of the times when the potatoes rotten. 'You paid no least heed,' she said."[31]

Do we pay heed to the world around us? Our world, our environment, is in such pain. Our physical world is connected to the spiritual realm. Yes, we need to take practical, concrete actions to help our physical world. But the role of the spiritual should not be neglected. What would our world look like if everyone returned to God, loved God and neighbor, respected God's name, and kept the Lord's Day holy? It isn't too late.

Our Blessed Mother still weeps for us. She wants us to return to her Son. Will we answer her plea?

PRAYERS TO OUR LADY OF LA SALETTE

Our Lady of La Salette, reconciler of sinners, pray without ceasing for us who have recourse to thee.

The Memorare to Our Lady of La Salette

Remember, Our Lady of La Salette, true Mother of Sorrows, the tears which thou didst shed for me on Calvary; be mindful also of the unceasing care which thou dost exercise to shield me from the justice of God; and consider whether thou canst now abandon thy child, for whom thou hast done so much. Inspired by this consoling thought, I came to cast myself at thy feet, in spite of my infidelity and ingratitude. Reject not my prayer, O Virgin of reconciliation, convert me, obtain for me the grace to love Jesus Christ above all things and to console thee too by living a holy life, in order that one day I may be able to see thee in Heaven. Amen.

NOTES

[1] Mary Hansen, "Weeping Mother: Our Lady of La Salette Calls for Prayer and Repentance in the Alps", *National Catholic Register*, May 12, 2019.

[2] Msgr. John S. Kennedy, *Light on the Mountain: The Story of La Salette* (New York: McMullen Books, 1953) 15.

[3] Kennedy, 15.

[4] Fr. Emile A. Ladouceur, M.S., *The Vision of La Salette: The Children Speak*, editor Fr. Ron Gagne, M.S. (Hartford: Missionaries of La Salette Corporation, 2016) 25.

[5] Ladouceur, 31.

[6] "La Salette: The Message and Its Meaning", https://www.lasalette.org/about-la-salette/apparition/the-story/705-the-message-of-la-salette.html

[7] Ladouceur, 81.

[8] Ladouceur, 67.

[9] Kennedy, 48.

[10] Kennedy, 74, 62.

[11] Kennedy, 92.

[12] Kennedy, 147.

[13] Kennedy, 140.

[14] James P. O'Reilly, M.S., The Story of La Salette: Its History and Sequels, (Techny, Illinois: Divine Word Publications, 1953) 122.

[15] O'Reilly, 126.

[16] Kennedy, 182-183.

[17] *The La Salette Controversy – Part VI*, http://www.salvemariaregina.info/SalveMariaRegina/SMR-171/LaSalette6.htm

[18] I debated including the text of this longer secret here, but decided it was best not to give something so questionable additional publicity. For those who wish to read it, please visit: http://www.miraclehunter.com/marian_apparitions/approved_apparitions/lasalette/secret-of-our-lady-of-lasalette-to-melanie-1879.html

[19] Mark Wyatt, *La Salette Secrets II*, http://veritas-catholic.blogspot.com/2006/08/la-salette-secrets-ii.html

[20] *The Secrets of La Salette*, https://www.michaeljournal.org/articles/roman-catholic-church/item/the-secrets-of-la-salette

[21] Both the original French and translated English versions may be found at: http://patristica.net/La-Salette&f&e

[22] Ladouceur, 42.

[23] Ladouceur, 45.

[24] Ladouceur, 52.

[25] Ladouceur, 52.

[26] O'Reilly, 52.

[27] O'Reilly, 51.

[28] O'Reilly, 163-164.

[29] Fr. Normand Theroux, M.S., *Our La Salette Mission: To Reconcile Her People With Her Son* (Attleboro, MA: La Salette Communications Center Publications, 2017).

[30] Theroux.

[31] Theroux.

ABOUT THE AUTHOR

Patrice Fagnant-MacArthur has a Master's Degree in Applied Theology. She is the author of The Catholic Baby Name Book and The Power of Forgiveness. She has also contributed articles to several online and print publications including CatholicMom.com, Catechist, Today's Catholic Teacher, and Catholic Library World.

A freelance writer and editor, she is also editor of TodaysCatholicHomeschooling.com. For more information, please visit pfmacarthur.com.

If you enjoyed this book, please consider leaving a review on Amazon.com, sharing with your social media channels, and telling your friends about it. Please help share Our Lady of La Salette's message with the world.

To find out more about Our Lady of La Salette, please visit www.lasalette.org.

Made in the USA
Monee, IL
26 March 2023

30580615R00035